Saving the Arctic

Serena Haines

Smithsonian

Contributing Author

Heather Schultz, M.A.

Consultants

William Fitzhugh
Senior Archaeologist
National Museum of Natural History

Tamieka Grizzle, Ed.D.
K–5 STEM Lab Instructor
Harmony Leland Elementary School

Stephanie Anastasopoulos, M.Ed.
TOSA, STREAM Integration
Solana Beach School District

Publishing Credits

Rachelle Cracchiolo, M.S.Ed., *Publisher*
Conni Medina, M.A.Ed., *Managing Editor*
Diana Kenney, M.A.Ed., NBCT, *Content Director*
Véronique Bos, *Creative Director*
Robin Erickson, *Art Director*
Seth Rogers, *Editor*
Mindy Duits, *Senior Graphic Designer*
Smithsonian Science Education Center

Image Credits: p.7 (bottom) Paul Nicklen/National Geographic Creative; p.8 Design Pics Inc/Alamy; pp.8–9 Ann Johansson/Corbis via Getty Images; p.9 (middle), p.17 (bottom), p.19 (bottom), p.22 © Smithsonian; p.10 (bottom) Accent Alaska.com/Alamy; pp.12–13 National Geographic Creative/Alamy; p.13 (top) Timothy J. Bradley; p.14 (bottom right) All Canada Photos/Alamy; p.16 Lawrence Migdale/Science Source; p.17 (top) Louise Murray/ Science Source; p.19 (top) RIA Novosti/Science Source; p.21 (top) Gunter Marx/Alamy; p.23 (all) NASA; p.27 (left) British Antarctic Survey/Science Source; p.27 (right) NOAA Climate Program Office, NABOS 2006 Expedition. Photo by Mike Dunn; p.32 (right) NASA's Goddard Space Flight Center/Kathryn Hansen; all other images from iStock and/or Shutterstock

Library of Congress Cataloging-in-Publication Data

Names: Haines, Serena author.
Title: Saving the Arctic / Serena Haines.
Description: Huntington Beach, California : Teacher Created Materials, [2019] | Includes index. | Audience: Grades: 4 to 6. |
Identifiers: LCCN 2018005252 (print) | LCCN 2018046856 (ebook) | ISBN 9781493869336 (E-book) | ISBN 9781493866939 (Paperback)
Subjects: LCSH: Arctic regions--Climate--Juvenile literature. | Climatic changes--Arctic regions--Juvenile literature. | Environmental responsibility--Juvenile literature.
Classification: LCC GB2595 (ebook) | LCC GB2595 .H35 2019 (print) | DDC 551.6911/3--dc23
LC record available at https://lccn.loc.gov/2018005252

Smithsonian

Teacher Created Materials
5301 Oceanus Drive
Huntington Beach, CA 92649-1030
www.tcmpub.com
ISBN 978-1-4938-6693-9

Printed by: 590835
Printed in: Taiwan

Table of Contents

At the Top of the World

Imagine you are looking at Earth from space. As you watch it rotate on its axis, you look north. It is covered in ice. You can see Greenland and the North Pole. That area at the top of the world is called the Arctic.

The Arctic is very important to our planet. It's like an air conditioning system for all of Earth!

Because Earth's **climate** is warming, ice in the Arctic is melting. As ice melts and seawater rises, more Arctic land disappears. People who live there have to **adapt** to new changes. So do animals that live there.

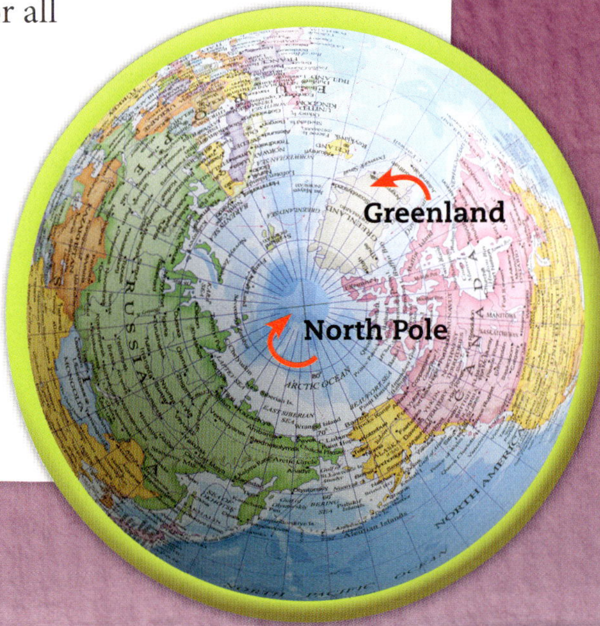

village in Greenland

Scientists go to the Arctic to study these changes. They may not be able to stop ice from melting, but they want to understand why it is melting so quickly.

They are also working closely with people from the Arctic. Together, they help write **policies** to reduce the harmful effects of climate change.

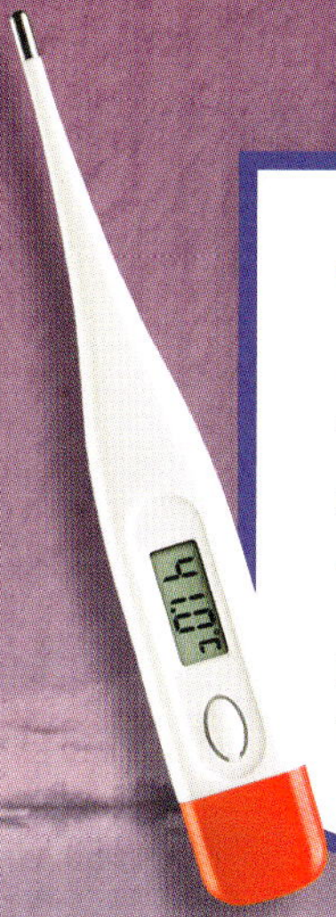

SCIENCE

Warming Up

Scientists keep track of Earth's temperatures. They compare them to the past. They have found that the average temperature has risen about 2° Celsius (3.6 Fahrenheit) in the last 150 years. Most of that change happened in the last 35 years. The Arctic is warming twice as much as the rest of the world.

Who Lives in the Arctic?

Even though it is one of the coldest places on Earth, the Arctic is home to many different animals. And there are about four million people who live there, too!

Arctic Animals

Polar bears, fish, seals, sharks, and whales all share this icy home. Some species can only be found in the Arctic. These species include polar bears and narwhals. Each narwhal has a long tooth called a tusk. A narwhal's tusk can grow to almost 2.7 meters (9 feet) long!

On land, **tundra** wolves stalk caribou. Arctic foxes hunt for food. Musk oxen feed on small tundra plants, and polar bears hunt for fish and seals in the water.

In the air, there are more than two hundred bird species. Snowy owls hunt for prey during the day. Arctic terns nest in the Arctic but **migrate** in the summer. Yellow-billed loons sing and call to each other.

All these animals make the Arctic their home. But as it gets warmer, they will have to adapt or they will go extinct.

seal

Caribou are the only type of deer in which both the male and female have antlers.

narwhals

Arctic People

The Yup'ik (YOO-pik) are a group of people who live on St. Lawrence Island off the coast of Alaska. They have lived on the frozen tundra for thousands of years. Yup'ik people are great at hunting and fishing. To cross ice, they use snowmobiles and dogsleds.

The people and animals of the Arctic plan their lives around weather. As it changes, it is harder to predict what each season will be like. How much rain will fall? How much ice will melt? It is important to be able to mark these changes.

Many different languages are spoken in the Arctic. The Yup'ik speak a language called Siberian Yup'ik. In Yup'ik, there are many words for "ice" and "snow." Until a few years ago, you would only hear those words if you talked to a native Yup'ik speaker. No one had written them down. Then, a scientist worked with a Yup'ik elder to make a "sea ice dictionary." Together they made a list of terms and what they mean in English. They added pictures, too. This list helps scientists talk with the Yup'ik. They can ask the Yup'ik what they see in the changing land.

The word *Yup'ik* means "real people."

Yup'ik Term	English Explanation
siku	the main term for ice; also, the ice-covered Bering Sea

A Yup'ik man stands near the coast of St. Lawrence Island.

The Science of the Arctic

Scientists all over the world study the Arctic. They look at the climate, land, people, and animals that live there.

Studying the Climate

How do people know the weather is getting warmer? **Climatologists** (klahy-muh-TAH-luh-jists) study weather. They collect data from samples they take from the air, water, and soil. Then, they look for patterns. In the Arctic, they get samples from ice cores and plants.

Scientists compare new data with data from the past. How does weather now compare to weather last month? How does it compare to last year or even the past hundred years? Trends show that average temperatures in the Arctic—and all over Earth—are getting higher.

It will keep getting warmer unless something changes. In fact, scientists believe it is warming faster than ever.

Climatologists test ice samples.

TECHNOLOGY

Powering Climate Stations

To study the climate of different regions, scientists set up remote climate stations. These stations observe and record temperature all the time. It can be a challenge to get power to these stations because of the weather. It can get as cold as –40°C (–40°F)! Special technology is used to keep the power going. Some stations have solar panels to use the power of the sun. Some use chemical fuel cells so that there can still be power when there is not much light.

solar panel

Arctic weather station

Studying the Land

How does the changing climate affect land and ice? That is what many different types of scientists are trying to find out.

Glaciologists (gley-shee-AH-luh-jists) study glaciers, icebergs, and sea ice. They learn about the ice and how fast it is melting.

Geologists study the earth and soil. They also study **permafrost**. Many homes in the Arctic are built on this frozen soil. As ice melts and flows into the ocean, it takes some soil with it. This is called **erosion**. As land erodes, people and animals have less land to live on.

Polar biologists study Arctic animals. They look at how animals are adapting to warmer weather. For example, polar bears need sea ice to travel and to hunt seals. Seals live and rest on sea ice. As ice melts, both seals and polar bears have to change their ways.

A glaciologist stands in a cave made mostly from ice.

ENGINEERING

Kite Sledding

Scientists in Greenland wanted a way to travel across ice that would not harm the environment. So, they built a sled that is pulled by a giant kite! It's called the WindSled, and it has been used on seven trips across the Greenland ice. It has traveled more than 19,300 kilometers (12,000 miles) so far! The sled weighs just over 1.8 metric tons (2 tons). It can hold up to six people, and it moves about 9.7 km per hour (6 mi. per hour).

A polar bear reaches into the water from a sheet of ice.

Studying the Animals and Plants

The Arctic Ocean is full of life! Fish, seals, polar bears, and many plants all live in and around the icy Arctic waters. It is the only place where some of the animals and plants can be found. And some are now **endangered species**. Scientists want to study them while they still can.

Marine biologists study the plants and animals that live in the Arctic Ocean. They look at what Arctic animals eat. They note which plants are no longer there.

Marine ecologists (ih-KAH-luh-jists) study the Arctic **ecosystem**. Plants, animals, and the nonliving things around them work together. Changes to nonliving things in an ecosystem can affect their food web. For example, fish eat plants in the water. Seals eat the fish. Polar bears eat the seals. If the plants die because of changes in the water, fish will have nothing to eat. They have to move to a new area. Then, seals and polar bears will have less to eat. Everything in the Arctic is connected!

Scientists study an Arctic fox.

ARTS

An Icy Vision

James Balog is a photographer who loves science. He founded the Extreme Ice Survey (EIS) program. It uses art and science to show how the climate is changing. EIS has placed dozens of cameras on glaciers. The cameras take pictures every hour of every day. Then, EIS uses those photos to make videos that show ice melting over time. James says these videos are giving a "voice" to the melting glaciers. Sometimes, a picture really is worth a thousand words!

Studying the People

Scientists also study people of the Arctic, such as the **Inuit** people. Scientists want to know more about their lives. They study how the Inuit hunt, what they eat, and where they live.

Ethnologists (eth-NAH-luh-jists) study the culture of people. Culture is made up of the traditions and customs of a group of people. What kind of houses do people live in? What do they eat? How are their lives changing as the climate gets warmer? Ethnologists try to find answers to these questions.

Archaeologists (ahr-kee-AH-luh-jists) in the Arctic study **artifacts** to find out what life was like long ago. At the site of an ancient house, they found a piece of a basket. It was more than 8,000 years old. They also found some pieces of driftwood. The wood came from hundreds of miles away. Scientists think a river carried the wood down to the house site. Then, the Inuit used the wood to build their homes. These artifacts are all clues to how Inuit people lived thousands of years ago.

Inuit children today

Inuit hunters haul a shark.

Inuit people wear clothing made of animal fur. They need layers of clothing to stay warm in the extreme cold.

animal fur coat

A Changing Land

Imagine you and your family have lived in the same place for generations. Even your great-great-grandparents once lived there. You would probably know a lot about that place. That is how the Inuit people feel about their home. They can tell when things change.

One Inuit elder told scientists that the weather was *uggianaqtuq* (OOG-ghee-ah-nahk-took). That is an Inuit word. It means, "behaving in an unexpected way."

The Arctic people are **eyewitnesses** to changes in the climate. They are used to changes in the weather. But what they have seen over the last few years has worried them.

The Inuit want to know why things are changing so fast. They are sharing what they have seen with scientists. Scientists call the data they get from the Inuit "traditional knowledge." Together, they hope to learn why the climate is changing. They want to know how to help slow the warming, too.

During summer in the Arctic, the sun shines 24 hours a day. This is why the Arctic is sometimes called the "Land of the Midnight Sun."

an Inuit family

Two men work at an Inuit settlement in 1924.

The Arctic people depend on the land every day. Changing weather has changed the way the Inuit live. When seasons come later in the year, caribou come later, too. People need to hunt caribou for food.

Many Inuit use ice for drinking water. When there was ice available all year, they could count on plenty of water to drink. But now that temperatures are warmer, they cannot be sure there will be enough.

Many homes in the Arctic are built on permafrost. As it gets warmer, the permafrost melts. The ground becomes soft and mushy. This can damage the houses and buildings above it. It can even cause landslides.

As ice melts into the sea, waves are given more space to grow bigger and stronger. When they crash on the shore, they take some of the soil back into the ocean. This speeds the process of erosion even more.

These bags of gravel slow erosion along the shoreline.

Warmer weather is raising the sea level and eroding the land along one-fourth of the Arctic coastline.

caribou

One reason the Arctic stays so cold is because of all the white snow and ice! The color white reflects the sunlight. The dark colors of the ocean and land absorb heat. As more ice melts, more land and sea are exposed. Those dark areas absorb more heat, which in turn melts more snow and ice.

This is why the rate at which the ice is melting is increasing. The more ice melts, the faster the rest of the ice melts. This makes it warmer, and then even more ice melts!

As sea ice melts, it also makes room for more ships to travel through the Arctic. More ship traffic means a higher chance of oil pollution. More pollution puts even more stress on the Arctic ecosystem.

How much ice is melting? Scientists say that more than 259,000 square km (100,000 square mi.) of summer sea ice is lost every 10 years. That is about the size of the state of Arizona!

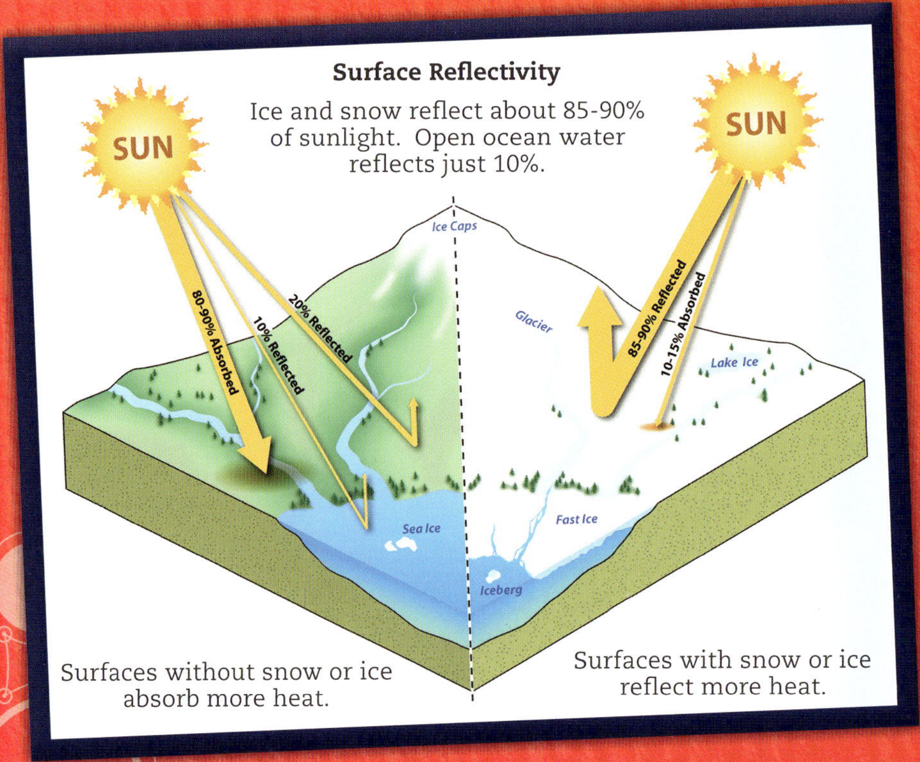

MATHEMATICS

By the Numbers

Climatologists use math to figure out how fast Arctic ice is melting. They measure the ice and collect data over time. They even use satellite pictures to see the changes from above. Then, they compare all the averages from each year on a graph to see the changes.

Arctic in 1984

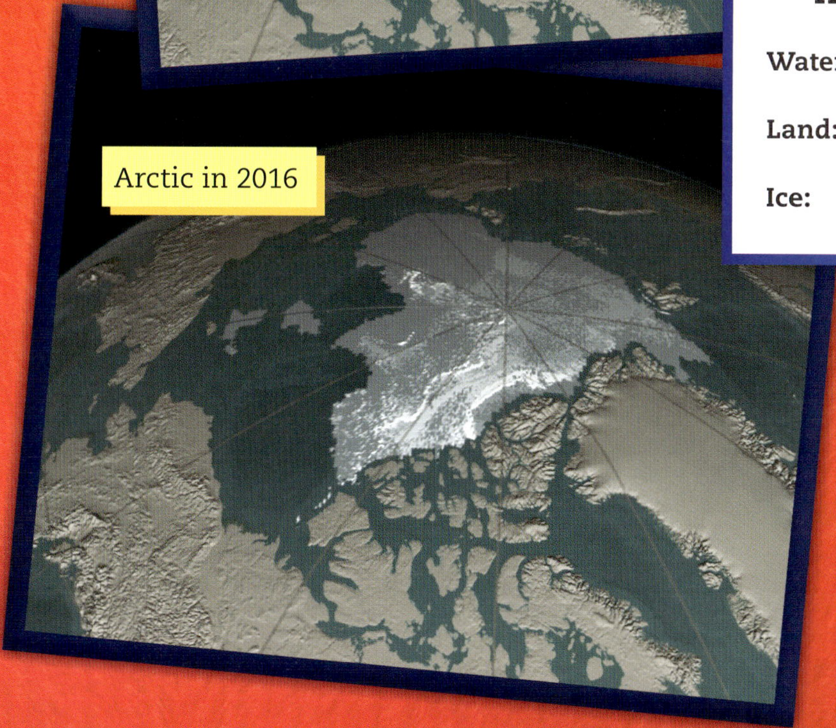

Arctic in 2016

Key:

Water:

Land:

Ice:

The Rest of the World

Earth depends on the Arctic to keep water temperatures cool. As the Arctic gets warmer, oceans are thrown out of balance. Water temperatures rise. Warmer water leads to warmer air. Then, it gets warmer everywhere.

Even small changes in temperature can cause big changes for the planet. When it gets even a little warmer, the weather gets more extreme. Storms, hurricanes, and heat waves happen more often and get stronger.

This extreme weather also affects farms. Too much or too little rain makes it harder for fruits and vegetables to grow. This means that more people will go hungry. Changes at the top of the world affect the whole planet. This is why people all over are working together to save the Arctic.

Some scientists say that summer sea ice may be completely gone by 2037.

A polar bear stands on a shrinking part of Arctic ice.

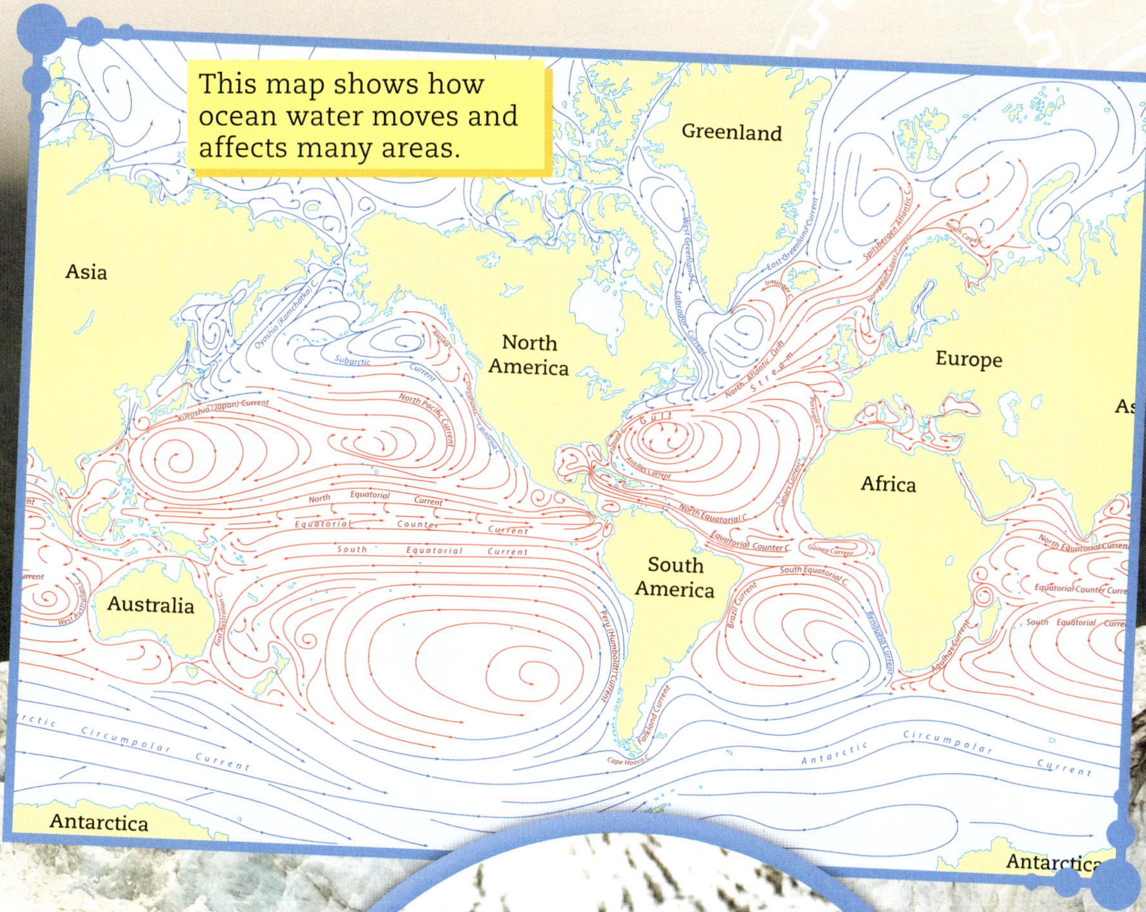

This map shows how ocean water moves and affects many areas.

A farmer looks at plants ruined by extreme weather.

Finding Solutions

How can people save the Arctic? One way is to use fewer **fossil fuels**. When people use these fuels, such as oil, coal, and natural gas, they damage the atmosphere. And fossil fuels are not renewable. That means that once they are gone, they are gone forever. People cannot make more.

Instead, people can use more energy powered by nature. What can be used to make power? Wind, water, and even the sun! These are called "clean" energies.

Scientists are using new technology to make clean energy sources even better. Then, more people around the world can use clean energy. That means there would be less damage to the atmosphere. It also means that the warming can be slowed.

Solar panels and wind turbines provide clean energy.

Polar scientists continue to study the Arctic. They use science and technology to work toward a solution. With the help of the Inuit, they hope to find more ways to save the Arctic. Everyone can help by learning more about why Earth is warming. Together, we can help protect the Arctic and the world.

Scientists collect and cut ice samples for study.

Sweden is working to become the first nation to be fossil-fuel free.

STEAM CHALLENGE

Define the Problem

When permafrost melts, the ground becomes soft and mushy. This sometimes damages houses and buildings built on it. Your task is to create a model house that can withstand melting of permafrost.

Constraints: The base of your house must fit inside a cake pan. It must weigh at least a $\frac{1}{2}$ kilogram (1 pound).

Criteria: Your house must remain upright, level, and undamaged as the permafrost melts.

1 Research and Brainstorm

What happens when frozen soil melts? What types of materials could provide support in multiple weather conditions? Will you need to add any extra supports to your structure?

2 Design and Build

Sketch a model of your house. Decide what materials will work best. Build your model.

3 Test and Improve

Place your model in a cake pan filled with frozen mud or ice. Place it under a heat lamp or out in the sun. Observe the movement of the building as the frozen layer begins to melt. Did your structure move? Did your structure become damp or weakened? Modify your design and try again.

4 Reflect and Share

What materials worked best? How might a building that was built on actual permafrost act differently than your model? Consider other solutions. Which might work best?

Glossary

adapt—make changes to adjust to new conditions

artifacts—objects made by humans from ancient times

climate—weather over time

climatologists—scientists who study the climate

ecosystem—the groups of living and nonliving things that make up an environment

endangered species—plants or animals that have become rare and could die out completely

erosion—the movement of weathered rock and sediment

ethnologists—scientists who study people and culture

eyewitnesses—people who see something firsthand, in person

fossil fuels—nonrenewable energy sources, such as oil, coal, and natural gas

glaciologists—scientists who study snow, ice, and glaciers

Inuit—the native people of the Arctic

marine biologists—scientists who study the ocean and everything that lives in it

migrate—to pass from one place to another in a repeating pattern

permafrost—frozen soil that contains mostly frozen water

policies—sets of accepted rules about what should be done

tundra—refers to a flat, frozen area with no trees

Index

CAREER ADVICE
from Smithsonian

Do you want to study the Arctic?
Here are some tips to get you started.

"You play a major role in solving Earth's problems. Little things help. Keep track of the places you go in a normal week and how you get there. Then, try to decrease the number of times you ride in a car to go places. Instead, walk or ride a bike. You can play an even bigger role by choosing a career in science, history, and technology. Find what interests you and learn all you can."—
William Fitzhugh, Museum Curator

"Human activities may be affecting temperatures and animals at both poles. Even if you do not live near the Arctic or Antarctica, you can still make a difference with your everyday actions. Learn about science and math. Invent new technology. Find artistic solutions to change the world."—
Emily Frost, Ocean Portal Managing Editor